# The A2Z of
## Early Childhood Management

# The A2Z of Early Childhood Management

An easy to read guide that has 26 proven management techniques that will put you and your staff on the road to success.

Insightful Strategies That Work.

Latorie S. Lloyd/ Synovia Dover-Harris, MBA

iUniverse, Inc.
Bloomington

**THE A2Z OF EARLY CHILDHOOD MANAGEMENT**
An easy to read guide that has 26 proven
management techniques that will put you
and your staff on the road to success.

Copyright © 2012 by Latorie S. Lloyd/ Synovia Dover-Harris, MBA.

Dr. Shirley B. Lloyd editor

All rights reserved. No part of this book may be used or reproduced by any means, graphic, electronic, or mechanical, including photocopying, recording, taping or by any information storage retrieval system without the written permission of the publisher except in the case of brief quotations embodied in critical articles and reviews.

iUniverse books may be ordered through booksellers or by contacting:

iUniverse
1663 Liberty Drive
Bloomington, IN 47403
www.iuniverse.com
1-800-Authors (1-800-288-4677)

Because of the dynamic nature of the Internet, any web addresses or links contained in this book may have changed since publication and may no longer be valid. The views expressed in this work are solely those of the author and do not necessarily reflect the views of the publisher, and the publisher hereby disclaims any responsibility for them.

Any people depicted in stock imagery provided by Thinkstock are models, and such images are being used for illustrative purposes only.
Certain stock imagery © Thinkstock.

ISBN: 978-1-4697-7904-1 (sc)
ISBN: 978-1-4697-7905-8 (ebk)

Printed in the United States of America

iUniverse rev. date: 04/10/2012

# CONTENTS

Introduction ........................................................................ vii
Why you need this book! ................................................... ix
A2Z Business Management for Childcare ... ................... xi
    For the Aspiring Childcare Director- ........................... xi
    For the New Childcare Directors: .................................. xii
    For the Experienced Childcare Directors: ................... xiii
A- Attitude ........................................................................... 1
B- Believe ............................................................................. 2
C- Chain of Command ....................................................... 3
D- Driver .............................................................................. 4
E- Experience ...................................................................... 5
F- Familiarize ...................................................................... 6
G- Gain ................................................................................. 7
H- Humor ............................................................................ 8
I- Invest ................................................................................ 9
J- Journal ........................................................................... 10
K- Know ............................................................................. 11
L- Leadership .................................................................... 12
M- Marketing .................................................................... 13
N- Nominate ..................................................................... 14
O- Organize ....................................................................... 15
P- Professionalism ............................................................ 16
Q- Quick ............................................................................ 17
R- Reputation .................................................................... 18
S- Support .......................................................................... 19
T- Time management ...................................................... 20
U- Unity ............................................................................. 21
V- Variety .......................................................................... 22
W- Wisdom ....................................................................... 23
X- Xenagogue (Guide) ..................................................... 24
Y- Your employees are #1! .............................................. 25
Z- Zappy; ........................................................................... 26

# Introduction

Statistics show that over 12 million children receive some type of childcare services and without a doubt all of these children are in situations where great management techniques are needed.

Great management techniques include, but are not limited to, proper training, years of experience, and educational tools.

High turnover within the childcare industry can be common in the classrooms and in the management field. One of the reasons this may occur is because of lack of knowledge and understanding of what really needs to be done to run a successful childcare center or school.

Whether it is a home base, religious, registered, or licensed childcare facility, the important and basic techniques must be mastered to operate a center successfully.

This guide will give you 26 proven management techniques that will improve your childcare management experience emotionally, professionally, and physically.

# Why you need this book!

What makes A2Z of Early Childhood Management services a unique comparison to other childcare guides:

- This is a simple and easy to read guide for all current and future members of management.
- This guide is useful for the early childhood college student.
- This guide provides a breakdown of information that will assist in the daily operation of any school.
- This guide can be used as an operational tool for a childcare director who has less than one year of childcare experience.
- This guide can be used as an inspirational tool for a seasoned director who has numerous years of childcare experience.

# A2Z Business Management for Childcare...

**For the Aspiring Childcare Director-**

The number one question in childcare for all employees is; "Why are you here?" Working with small children can be a challenge. The love and nurturing component that you have from within will always make your job rewarding! Having a love for children is the overall key to succeeding in the field for early childhood education.

A2Z of Early Childhood Management provides you with the basic introduction of childcare management as well as information that you can use throughout the industry. This tool could be used to assist in your growth within the industry as well as contribute towards your leadership development. Leadership positions in childcare centers can be challenging: However, with consistency, discipline, and structure, you can become very successful in this field.

### For the New Childcare Directors:

The average childcare center operates with an enrollment of 50 children or more and an average of 15 teachers. As a childcare director, you are responsible for the full daily operation of the center in which you are employed.

It is important that you have a full understanding of your position, in addition to your job description and responsibilities.

The childcare director's position can be overwhelming without the proper training, guidance, tools, and support.

A2Z of Early Childhood Management provides you with some keys to succeeding in your position. It is clearly up to you, the reader, to use this key to contribute towards your success.

Allow A2Z of Early Childhood Management to be the inspirational tool that will encourage you along your successful journey as a childcare director in the early childhood field.

### For the Experienced Childcare Directors:

Directors are considered the hearts of many child-care centers. The director often sets the tone of love, dedication, and professionalism within their environment. Director's turnover on any level of childcare can be detrimental to the operation of the business. As directors, operators, and owners, we are exposed to many burdens in our positions.

It is very easy to lose track of our goals, become overburdened, and even burned out. Allow this tool to give you the opportunity to revive, reflect, and revisit your current operational systems.

This inspirational tool provides you with information that will motivate you to step outside your comfort zone and take your center to the next level successfully.

It is often said that seasoned childcare directors become complacent in their positions. Allow A2Z of Early Childhood Management to lead and motivate you, and guide your center and team into a new direction that would benefit children who you love and provide care for every day.

A2Z of Early Childhood Management is a management guide for anyone who is in the childcare industry, thinking about going in the childcare industry, or need to revamp their current management style.

This guide will give effective, life-long lessons about the importance of positive and productive management techniques in an Early Childhood environment.

Inspiring children in a consistent
and professional environment adds value
to the life of every child.

Latorie S. Lloyd

# ttitude

*Your attitude speaks volume!*

As an early childhood educator maintaining a professional image is extremely important for your career and your success within your childcare facility.

According to Webster, attitude is defined as a mental position; and the feeling one has for oneself.

Your attitude represents who you are when you approach new parents, employees, and children. Your attitude will also influence the structure of your team.

Presenting an optimistic attitude throughout the center will foster an upbeat and positive environment for everyone. Your team will feed off of your attitude.

There will be situations when maintaining a professional composure will be difficult. It is up to you to maintain the appropriate attitude, so you will reflect a professional image at all times. Write down a set of professional values that you have created for yourself and be sure to include those values in your work ethic.

This practice will assist in building your professional image, which will speak volumes about your attitude.

# Believe

*"Believe in yourself that you can succeed at your job."*

Establishing confidence in yourself is a key to succeeding in this career.

You must always believe in yourself. To believe in yourself, begin by asking yourself the number one question . . . is this job for me? Working with children can be difficult if your heart is not in this field. Approach each day with the mind set that you are going to do your best. Each day will grow into a new accomplishment and over a period of time you will be able to visually see your success! Build your confidence from the foundation of "yes, this is for me and I will do the best that I can do."

This may seem like a simple statement, but when you are faced with challenging situations it is easy to lose confidence in yourself and what you believe in. As a childcare professional, you must believe that everything you do is for the good of all children you serve.

Always make sure your beliefs are parallel to your companies' belief and mission. When the two reflect upon each other the outcome of your production will turn out great!

# Chain of Command

*"Be knowledgeable of the chain of command in your business."*

The Chain of Command is considered the ranking of reputable positions within a company. For large businesses, the chain of command can begin with the director and go as high as a CEO! For smaller businesses the chain of command can be the director and/or the owner.

The first tools to become familiar with are the policies & procedures, the chain of command, and the grievance policy within your company.

The Chain of Command must be respected when reporting grievances. It is the director's responsibility to ensure that all employees under their leadership have a clear understanding of the chain of command and all policies. You will eliminate a host of confusion by making sure your employees are clear on these policies.

It is highly recommended to include this information in your new hire orientation and revisit these policies frequently during employee meetings.

Always keep this component of the business professional, regardless of which role you represent in any situation.

# Driver

*"Know that you are the driver of your school"*

It all begins with you!! You are the driver of your school. Understand that you are the person who sets the tone for your environment. When the opportunity is present to tour a new family, it is your persona that sells the business. If you are excited about your school, your program, and your teachers, you will excel in pleasing the parents.

Providing top notch customer service is a great tool for the success of your school. Excellent customer service is not limited to new enrollees. As the driver of your program, customer service extends to your current families, vendors, the community, and your employees.

As the director, create an environment that says "I want to be here and so do you." This will encourage visitors to return for enrollment and it will also excite families and employees who come into the school daily.

There will be times when the mood of the environment will be challenged. It is up to you, the driver, to take advantage of the opportunity to intervene promptly and quickly to bring your school's environment back to where it belongs.

# Experience

*"Bring all of your experience to the table"*

Experience is a great tool when working in an early childhood setting. Experience begins when you first start working with children. Positive experience as well as negative experience can be used and applied throughout your career. Bringing all of your experiences to the table means you bring everything that you have learned over the years through trial and error and use that knowledge as an asset to your school.

If you are new to the early childhood field, you may also incorporate previous life and work experiences and apply them as you see necessary.

Know how to create a balance with your life and work experiences so that you will be highly effective in your position.

*For example: The love, care, and respect you express to your immediate family members can also be the same love, care, and respect that you offer your children and employees.*

If you have years of experience in this field, take time to reflect back to when you started. Use those memories as a tool to mentor and lead your team.

# Familiarize

*"Familiarize yourself with the business of the current school."*

Every school has its own unique culture! When beginning employment in a new environment, take time to learn detailed information about that school. It is recommended that you go in and learn about the operations already in place and its history, before making any changes. Communicate with current employees to discover what works and obtain their perceptions on what changes are needed. During this process, make continuous notes so that you may reflect on what needs to be revised, implemented, and/or removed.

Operating a business is a challenging task, so take your time intertwining into the culture of the school and gradually implement the changes that you see are necessary for the success of your school. Prioritize and set goal dates for the changes that you have decided to implement. It is also recommended to research the financial history of the school. By doing this, you are learning where you stand, financially, in the beginning so that you may reflect upon the growth and/or decrease over various time periods. Familiarizing yourself with the business of your current school will contribute to how you set goals for the future success of your school.

# ain

*"Gain a positive reputation for your school in your community."*

Gain a positive image for yourself and your school in the community in which your school is located. Begin this process by networking with businesses that are near your school. You can start by introducing yourself to other business, find out what they are offering, and give them a little insight about your business.

Stay informed about events that are scheduled in your community and be sure to attend at least 50 percent of those functions. By doing this, you are becoming a familiar face to other business members and you are supporting their functions. Most businesses will welcome your support, and in return, they will attend your functions to offer their support. Always keep business cards on you at all times. Most marketing opportunities occur during community functions or at the spur of the moment.

Involve yourself in volunteer opportunities that contribute to the uplifting of the school's community and benefit children you serve. Get to know your competitors in the area and form a networking relationship. Obtain a positive name for yourself and your school by presenting a level of respect for yourself and your business with the members of your community.

# umor

*"Experience humor each day by remembering to have fun!"*

What fun is all work and no play? *"We are Early Childhood Professionals . . . we have an excuse to have fun!!!*

Always remember why you initially chose to work in the Early Childhood field. Working with children can be such a joy if you allow yourself to seize the moment. Every day is always going to be different. Bring humor to your school by hosting fun teambuilding activities with your employees during working hours. When your employees enjoy themselves at work, they will spread that joy with the children in their classrooms. This type of joy will reflect the culture of the entire environment. Having humor each day also cuts back on the level of stress members in management can sometimes encounter. Humor assists in the management of your team because it cuts back on their level of stress as well. A fun icebreaker is a great way to start your monthly employee meetings. This relaxes the atmosphere and gets everyone prepared for a remarkable and rejuvenating meeting. Pick and chose your battles by finding humor in the challenging tasks that presents itself on a day-to-day basis. Make time to experience humor joyfully each day by remembering to plant the seed for fun in your professional environment.

# Invest

*"Invest in education and additional training"*

Although the average owner, operator, and director may have years of experience in early childhood education, it is recommended that all members of management (and teachers) invest in some form of formal education.

Many childcare regulatory systems are requiring leaders in early childcare facilities to obtain a degree or credential, that is relevant in early childhood.

Understanding growth and development as well as the logic behind children's cognitive development will assist in fostering a positive and stimulating learning environment for all children under your leadership.

All employees on your team who work directly with children should complete the basic early childhood education course. Be sure to keep yourself and your employees up to date annually on trainings and workshops that are relevant to each position. As laws, regulations, educational information, and statistics change, you must stay knowledgeable so that you are operating within compliance and providing children at your school with quality services.

See the list of recommend training on pages 34 and 38.

# ournal

*"Keep a journal for important notes and occurrences."*

Everyone has heard the phrase *"we are only human"*. It is very easy to lose track or forget information. Directors and other members of management wear a lot of hats during the course of a day and things may happen that we may not remember.

A journal can consist of a one subject spiral notebook that you can purchase at the local store for approximately one dollar. In your journal, write the date and time along with each note. Highlight the dates and or the main subjects that you need to reference to assist in keeping track of your information.

*For example; the child's name (Star Harris), the vendor (Lloyd's catering), the event (Christmas Party 2015) or the teachers name (Michael Brown) etc.*

If a thought occurs and you need to make a note of something, be sure to write it in your journal. Your journal can become a great reference tool when you are faced with a variety of situations and you are unable to recall specific details. Also use your journal to write goals, ideas, and upcoming events. Once you have exhausted your space in the journal, label it using the date of the first entry *(January 1, 2022)* to the date of the last entry *(December 31, 2022)* and store it in a safe and confidential location.

# now

*"Have confidence by Knowing that you are the best at what you do!"*

Knowing that you are the best at what you do is a dynamic force to your success. Having confidence within yourself, your position, and your school will be a key factor in selling your program.

When you express confidence to your team, their level of respect for you will consistently remain at a high level. Having confidence is also a form of mentoring. Your level of confidence will also assist in building your team's assurance.

Confidence is a great marketing tool. When you are touring your school or speaking to someone about your program, your level of confidence will send positive vibes that will help you sell your business.

When you are prioritizing your professional goals, the first thing you need to ask yourself is *"Am I 100 percent confident in my position?"* If you are not, then it is recommended that you map out a plan so you may obtain the confidence needed to know that you are the best at what you do.
*For example: Take extra training classes or read a book like this one.*

# Leadership

*"To be a leader, you need to inspire your team to follow."*

According to sources, leadership is defined as the process of social influence in which one person can enlist the aid and support of others in the accomplishment of a common task.

To be a leader, you must have the ability to inspire others. Create a vision that your team members are excited to follow.

*Leadership is not about being the "boss."*

Every member of management must know that they are not able to operate a business alone. To operate a successful school, a leader puts together a powerful team that will assist in accomplishing the goals that the program offers. I have often referenced Director's as the head (body part) of the center. Yes, you are the leader; however, without arms and legs, you will not be able to move forward. Your team represents your arms and legs. If they are not moving toward the goals that you have envisioned, your vision will perish. There are a host of books available on leadership (A2Z of Leadership) that will provide you with guidance on leading your team. Inspiring your team to join you in your vision will take your school to a successful level.

# Marketing

*"You are marketing your school at all times."*

You are constantly marketing your school and it is not limited to traditional advertising. Your largest clientele is your current enrolled families. The number one marketing tool in the childcare industry is word of mouth.

Marketing within your school consist of providing excellent customer service to your current families. Prospective parents who tour your facility are referred there by current families and/or someone in the community who is familiar with your program. Marketing also consist of making public appearances in the community. It is recommended that you keep your business cards, flyers, and all promotional items on you at all times. The best marketing opportunity presents itself when you least expect it. You may be eating lunch, shopping at the mall, or just getting gas at the gas station. Casual conversations can easily turn into a marketing opportunity for your program.

Remember to carry yourself in a professional manner at all times. It is your persona that sells your program as well. You are marketing your school at all times, even when you are putting in the least effort.

# Nominate

*"Nominate individuals on your team to assist in specific areas."*

As a member of management, you are not able to do everything. Motivate your teachers to be leaders by assigning them specific task in your facility. Before assigning responsibilities to your employees, observe each of them and learn their strengths and weaknesses.

By assigning these responsibilities to your employees, you are involving them in the growth of your school which leads toward the completion of your goals. Everyone will enjoy being a part of a growing project and a successful team. When you assign responsibilities, you are telling them that you trust them, you are confident in them, and you are proud to have them on your team. It is recommended that you also pair up employees by creating teams based on strengths and weakness. Once you have assigned a task to an individual or a group, be sure to oversee the project and provide the appropriate feedback.

As a member of management, it is very easy to become overwhelmed. Delegating different tasks to your team will lighten your load, involve your employees, and encourage leadership.

# rganize

*"Make sure your system remains organized."*

Many times you may walk into an office and someone will say, "Trust me; there is a method to this madness." Everyone has an organized system in place. Ask yourself these questions:

1. Is your system effective?
2. Does your system consist of searching through papers on the left or right side of your desk?
3. If you need to take vacation for a week, can someone step in and operate your system?

Maintaining an organized system means your "method of madness" does not only work for you. Create a system that is effective for the operation of the business. When operating a school, one day can be calm, whereas, the next day may not be as smooth. Three-ring binders are a great tool to use in childcare facilities. Create a filing system on your desk for items that needs to be filed verses putting everything into one stack. Dedicate your entire day to that specific project. When you are working on several projects, it is easy to jump back and forth between the projects. When this happens, something always falls short. Try to establish a habit of completing a project before moving on to the next. Maintaining an organized system benefits you by keeping your level of stress at a minimum.

# Professionalism

*"Maintain a professional environment in your school at all times."*

Directors maintain a professional environment when they lead by example. Leading by example means you are modeling a level of professionalism that raises the integrity at your school. As stated before under the letter L, the leader in the facility sets the tone for the school. Professionalism in a leader does not only entail your attitude, it also reflects your appearance and the way you communicate. Your employees will follow your lead and respect you, as well as each other. Your environment will also sell your school. When your employees are communicating with families in a professional manner, it presents a respectable environment to parents and they become comfortable with leaving their children in your school. An environment that does not maintain an appropriate level of professionalism and appears to be "not together", will cause parents to eventually look for an alternate school that will provide their child with more stimulation and professionalism.

Establish clear policies and guidelines for your employees so that everyone is working towards maintaining a professional environment in your school.

# Quick

*"Always provide a quick response!"*

As the person in charge of the childcare facility, everyone turns to you for answers. There are many times when you will not have the answer to respond immediately. It is important that you provide a quick response for your employees and families.

Avoid saying *"I don't know"* and leaving questions unanswered. You are viewed as a leader in your facility and that response tells others that you are incompetent in your position. A respectable response would be, *"I will get that information for you by the end of the day"* or any positive response that is appropriate for the situation. Providing a quick response to negative situations is also needed. As a director, you are responsible for correcting a situation immediately (when appropriate). While walking through the facility, you may witness an employee doing something inappropriate. It is your duty to respond immediately to the situation by correcting the employee at that time. Having the ability to respond quickly to emergency situations in a calm manner is very important. Be sure to keep a list of phone numbers available and easily accessible in your office.

# Reputation

*Your professional and personal reputation will always follow you!"*

As the saying goes, *"If you have nothing else in this world, you have your name."* Your reputation in your business follows you professionally and personally.

When it comes to professional and personal reputation, there is a very thin line. It is easy for the two to intertwine, especially if you live and work in the same community. Your personal reputation will effect the operation of your business. As stated under the letter "M", your number one marketing tool is word of mouth. If members of the community are communicating negative information about you, the director/owner, then your business reputation will be in jeopardy. Negative marketing could be detrimental to your business. You must maintain a reputable status at all times. Always think ahead about the choices you make and how you communicate with others, both personally and professionally. Your persona will determine how you are viewed by families, employees, and members of the community. Your reputation affects the operation of your business because it can make or break the enrollment in your school. Branding your name is making it recognizable (SD, Harris, 2009). Always maintain professionalism when you are on social network sites and groups such as Facebook, Twitter, MySpace, and in-person networks and associations.

# Support

*"Establish a Support System."*

Establishing a positive support system is great for your sanity. As a director, you are going to be faced with many challenges. Involve yourself with people who you can trust and turn to when you need to vent your frustration. If you work for a company that has a large number of schools, team up with another school director so the two of you can motivate each other. For smaller companies, get to know other school directors within your area so you will have someone to communicate with who truly understands your position.

A support system should include people who are on the same level of professionalism. It is not advised to include your employees in your support system. Create a support system that includes people who are positive, encouraging, honest, and sincere. Those traits will be an important asset when you need support. When communicating with members in your support system, be very careful not to breach the confidentiality policy for your business. Members of your support system should be there for you when you need to talk and reach out for constructive opinions. You must remain professional at all times, even with our support team.

Create a list of people who can be a part of your support team who you can meet with accordingly.

# Time management

*"Having great time management skills will help you to be an effective and efficient director."*

Have you ever asked yourself, *"Where has the time gone?"* or said *"There are not enough hours in the day!"* Time management is a great tool for any member in management. For the director in a childcare facility, time management is a necessity. Each day is different when working with children and there are times when the schedule does not always go as planned. Establish a routine for yourself and allow it to be flexible on a day-to-day basis. Prioritize your task so you are clear on the importance of each task and set your time limit accordingly. Effective time management also limits the level of stress a director can accumulate while working in a childcare facility. When being faced with a variety of situations, you must pick and choose your battles. As directors, we sometimes place our focus and time in a particular situation entirely too long. This causes us to lose track of time. When you have effectively practiced time management, you will leave each day with a feeling of completion and will be prepared to face the next day.

Start each day with a 'to do' list so you will know what you are doing throughout the day. Items not completed on the list will be placed at the beginning of the list for the next day.

# Unity

*"Unify your team!"*

Unity means bringing everyone together on one accord.

When managing a child care facility, directors must unify their team as soon as possible. Have frequent meetings that provide employees with detailed information about your goals and visions for the school. Directors must also keep in mind that they are supervising unique individuals from different walks of life.

Be sure to include time for team building activities during monthly meetings and during working hours. If one employee out of ten is not in unity with the team, it can and will be detrimental to the operation of your school. It is advised not to place too much time into an employee who is resistant to your vision. Negativity can be contagious and one disgruntle employee can easily influence others on your team. It is recommended that you document and work toward replacing that employee with a positive and qualified team player.

When you have established unity within your school, it creates a strong team that will definitely succeed your expectations.

# Variety

*"Participate in a variety of events and activities."*

Everyone enjoys having fun. Involve your school in events and activities that bring variety to the environment. As educators in the early childhood field, we encourage children to be creative. By bringing different activities to your school environment, you are inspiring children, parents, and teachers, to be creative. Invite a variety of programs such as gymnastics, sports, dances, fundraisers, music lessons and cheerleading. Conduct research in your community to see if vendors are available to visit your school. Seasonal activities are also exciting for families and employees. Activities such as Spring and Fall Carnivals, Valentine Dances, Christmas programs, Thanksgiving dinners, and summer cook-outs are all fun activities that contribute towards the culture of your school.

When planning activities and events, be mindful of the different cultures, religions, and economic status of families enrolled your school. Prepare a budget that is cost effective for the school and/or families who are participating. Be excited when you introduce new activities and events to your families and employees. Your tone will set the stage for their participation.

# isdom

*"Always apply Wisdom when operating a business."*

What is knowledge without wisdom? Wisdom is having the ability to apply common sense to everyday situations.

You may have a certificate, associate's degree, a bachelor's degree, or even a master's degree placed on the wall in your office. However, if you do not have the wisdom to apply your knowledge to unique situations, you will struggle in your position.

Having wisdom is about knowing that every situation is going to be different as well as every response. Wisdom also comes from life's experiences. To be wise is being able to identify and accept the truth (negative or positive) and being able to move forward and grow from it. There may be times when you will react to a situation without thinking clearly, and perhaps not make the best decision.

That is a part of building your wisdom. If you encounter a similar situation in the future, you will be wise enough to know how to respond to it based on a previous experience.

Be wise in the choices you make for your school. Making wise choices will result in a successful operation of your school.

# Xenagogue (Guide)

*"Be the guide for your team"*

As the person in charge you definitely have to be the guide. Do not engage into anything that you would not want your employees to do. Your professional behavior is the model that your team will follow. It begins with you conducting yourself in a respectable manner and your team will fall in line. The Director is always on radar.

For example:
- If you want your staff to come to work on time, you must come to work on time.
- If you want your staff to use professional language at all times, you should use professional language at all times.
- If you do not want an environment full of gossip and chaos, you must never entertain meaningless conversations.
- Do not show favoritism among your employee. This teaches them how to communicate equally without relying on cliques.
- Dress in appropriate attire if you want your staff to dress appropriately.

Remember to guide your team with the same level of integrity that you expect them to contribute to the school.

# Your employees are #1!

As mentioned previously, when operating a school always keep in mind that you are not capable of running your school alone. Remember to show your employees your appreciation of their services and contributions.

When you have a team of employees who are fully focused and committed on the goals set for your school, the outcome alone will sell the school. It is the directors' job to sell the services you provide and enroll new students to the school. It is the employees who work hand in hand with children and parents ... who close the back door and retain the enrollment.

When your teachers are excited about implementing the program, their classrooms turns into a marketing tool for your school through word of mouth advertisements.

Appreciation can be shown to teachers through:
- Performance reviews
- Quick response to concerns
- Gifts and Gestures
- Recognition

By expressing gratitude consistently with your employees you are showing them that they are a priority and the #1 contributor to your program.

# Zappy;

No one wants to work in a boring and bitter environment. Making things lively and entertaining is a proven way to retain employees.

Being the person in charge puts you in the position of establishing a positive rapport.

Research shows that employees, who love their work environment, work harder and is more productive. They are loyal and more willing and to achieve organizational goals and the high levels of excellence you put in place.

Dedication is also apparent in a positive and zappy environment. Employees will think twice about putting themselves or co-workers in uncompromising positions. All actions are made consciously and clearly established.

Employees who do not care about one another do things that are selfish and demeaning. Maintaining a zappy environment discourages employees from performing selfish acts and encourages a lively environment.

## Required Documents:

- A current operating license. (posted in a visible location for everyone)
- Updated employees' records. (Placed in a secure and confidential location).
- Updated children's records. (Updated annually or when there is a change of information.)
- Updated policies, procedures, and bi-laws. (copies available for respectable parties)
- Child Care Regulatory Guidelines. (Must be readily available and reviewed often).
- Emergency Evacuation Plans. (In office and posted in all classrooms).

## Items to always have available:

- First aid kits readily available for each classroom and all means of transportation.
- Emergency Forms readily available for all enrolled children and employees.
- Emergency Services Contact information in open and clear view.
- Transportation policy with detailed information about how you are going to provide transportation for children you serve.
- Employees Policy and Procedure Handbook.
- Parent Policy and Procedure Handbook.
- Listing of various trainings available for you and your team.

## Important telephone numbers to have available:

- Local Fire Department
- Local Police Department
- Supervisor, Owner and/or Corporate Office
- All Active Employees
- Child Care Regulatory Office
- Poison Control Center
- Local Security System Monitoring Office

# The Daily Checklist:

- ✓ Maintain and check teacher: child ratios through-out the day. At a minimum every hour.
- ✓ Post and deposit tuition payments.
- ✓ Make sure menus are posted and changes are made when necessary.
- ✓ Greet and follow up with prospective and newly enrolled parents. (ex: phone call, e-mail, thank you card, etc.)
- ✓ Classrooms are orderly, clean and sanitized throughout the day and at the end of the day.
- ✓ Ensure that employees are professional in appearance.

## The Weekly Checklist:

- Charge weekly tuition and fees on Monday.
- Collect weekly payments from parents and guardians.
- Collect previous week's attendance sheets from classrooms.
- Update weekly menu for parents review.
- Complete employee schedules and monitor work time.
- Review immunization records and send home notices.
- Review parent accounts with tuition assistance for changes.

## The Monthly Checklist:

- School Newsletters
- Fire and Emergency Drills
- Employee Meetings
- Review newly enrolled documents for signatures and completion.
- Review employee records for assessments and expiration dates.
- Send letters to inactive families who may have a balance.
- Update monthly financial reports and records.

# The A2Z Successful Staff Meeting Guide:

1. Have an agenda and make sure you follow it.
2. Have all information you want to discuss readily available so you are not searching for it.
3. Paperwork that needs to be completed by your staff should be available at the point of discussion.
4. Remember to make your meeting active and involve your staff so they do not become bored. Stay away from negative conversations and topics.
5. Always ask open ended questions. This gives your staff an opportunity to respond.
6. Before closing, ask your staff if they have anything they want to discuss further, or if they have any questions.

## Recommended Training Areas:

- Leadership
- Child Care Management
- Business Management
- Team Building
- Customer Service
- Growth and Development for Early Childhood
- Understanding Finance and Budgets

## Marketing Materials:

- Flyers
- Business Cards
- Bookmarks
- Education/Enrollment literature
- Gift Bags (for newborns at hospitals)
- Refrigerator Magnets
- Auto Magnets
- Window Decals for parents and employees
- Road Signs
- Posters

And so much more... see A2Z Inspirational Marketing for additional ideas.

## Touring Your School:

- ❖ Have enrollment packets completed and available before the family arrives. Be sure to include your contact information and tuition rates in the packet.
- ❖ Greet the family at the door with a smile and a warm welcome. Introduce yourself and let them know your position in the school.
- ❖ Shake the family member(s) hands and get each name. Be sure to give the child special attention.
- ❖ Bring the family into your office and provide them with information about your program and your school. Ask the family if they have any questions before touring the building.
- ❖ Take the family on a tour, ending at the classroom their child will be attending.
- ❖ Introduce the teachers and give a brief history of each teacher. (Ex. Ms. Sims has been in the Early Childhood field for over six years.)
- ❖ Show the parents the highlights of the classroom. (Ex: Parent Board, Lesson Plans, Daily Schedule, etc.)
- ❖ Do not forget to close the tour by asking the family if they would like to enroll today or when would they like for their child to start. Be sure to inform them of the great promotions that you are offering at that time.
- ❖ The key is to not apply any pressure. They are not buying a car.... They are looking for quality care for their child or children.

Available Certified Training that correlates with A2Z of Early Childhood Management Industry:

- Incorporating Leadership in an Early Childhood Setting
- The KEYS to Success
- D.R.A.M.A. (Don't React All the time . . . Move Away)
- Dress to Impress!
- Getting the Right People on Board!
- Motivating Your Team

We hope that this guide has inspired you to successfully manage your childcare center effectively.

Remember your success in this industry will be determined by how hard you work to develop relationships with your parents, employees, the community, and the children you serve.

*"Successful management is leading by example. So do the right thing and the right people will follow!"*

*SD Harris*

Best Regards

Latorie S. Lloyd, BBA
Synovia Dover-Harris, MBA

Available A2Z Books:

➢ The A2Z of Success
➢ The A2Z of Inspirational Marketing

Books Coming Soon:

➢ The A2Z of Power
➢ The A2Z of Money Management
➢ The A2Z Relationship Series

www.ingramcontent.com/pod-product-compliance
Lightning Source LLC
Chambersburg PA
CBHW021042180526
45163CB00005B/2237